A PARENT'S GUIDE TO PSYCHOEDUCATIONAL EVALUATIONS

Paula Elitov, Ph.D.

ISBN: 978-1-09834-056-8 eBook 978-1-09834-057-5

CONTENTS

PREFACE

My goal in writing this book is to help parents who are about to begin the process of obtaining a psychoeducational evaluation for their child, make the process more meaningful, useful, and ultimately beneficial for their child. As I talk with parents who are about to begin this journey, I find that many are not familiar with what is involved, what the terms mean, what the tests are, and why we as evaluators recommend certain procedures.

A psychoeducational evaluation can vary greatly in the extent of testing and procedures, the way it is conducted, and the report that is created. Learning more about what choices are available and what contributes to a good evaluation is important for parents considering this type of assessment. In addition, after many years of doing psychoeducational evaluations with a wide variety of children, I believe that for some children, there are adaptations needed in the testing process and ways of gathering relevant information that are important in order to obtain meaningful results. Furthermore, it is important to challenge ourselves as evaluators to find ways to innovate with the output and presentation of results that contribute to better evaluations. My purpose in writing this book is to help parents become savvy about the testing process so that they can get more out of the evaluation and can more easily advocate for their child.

CHAPTER ONE

What's involved in a psychoeducational evaluation and does my child really need one?

Many parents are not sure what is involved in a psychoeducational evaluation and do not know what kind of testing would make sense. Some are not really sure whether an evaluation is even necessary. To help make this decision, parents may find it useful to have an initial conversation with a psychologist. This often takes place over the phone to start with. This preliminary discussion is a way for parents to share their concerns and learn a little more about what is involved in an evaluation. The psychologist, in turn, will likely ask questions that can help clarify whether an evaluation would be helpful and can describe what different types of assessments can offer.

Do these concerns warrant an evaluation?

Parents may initially be unsure about whether their concerns and observations warrant an evaluation. These questions may present differently based on the age of their child. Examples of concerns that often prompt parents to make an initial call to a psychologist are:

At the preschool level:

- "My child is not able to sit for circle time or group activities."

- "My four year old has not learned the names of colors, numbers or letters."

- "My child's teacher told me that my child tends to resist activities that involve drawing or writing."

- "My child is not able to engage in back and forth play with peers."

- "My child is very verbal but seems to avoid a lot of academic activities presented at school."

- "My child's language skills sound below average and I'm worried about readiness for kindergarten."

At the elementary school level:

- "The school has been calling about my child's behavior in class and is reporting excessive silliness, restlessness and attention-seeking behavior."

- "My child seems to struggle a great deal with homework."

- "I just received my child's report card and there are ratings that are below grade level in some areas and above grade level in others."

- "My child has social difficulty with peers and has trouble making friends."

- "The teacher has made comments that my child needs constant attention to get work done."

- "When responding to homework assignments, my child can easily verbalize a good answer, but then struggles to put these same ideas into writing."

- "My child will often learn a new concept but then seems to forget it the next time it is presented."

- "My child behaves well at school but then comes home and falls apart."

At the middle school or high school level:

- "Homework seems to take the whole evening when it should take an hour or two."

- "My child seems to be struggling with anxiety and depression and I want to find out how to provide appropriate support at school."

- "My child's written work is so simplistic and different from what he seems to be able to express orally."

- "My high school student can't finish tests in class with standard time."

- "With demands for extensive reading, my child seems to take a long time to read and then can't easily process what is read without support."

- "I had some minor concerns in elementary school, but now at the middle school (or high school) level, with so many classes and with more complex work demands, my child seems overwhelmed."

Based on these concerns, a psychologist will typically ask questions to clarify the nature of the concerns and to discuss with parents whether their questions suggest that a psychoeducational evaluation would be beneficial. If so, the psychologist can discuss how an evaluation could shed light on these concerns. This discussion is often helpful to parents in making a decision about whether they would like to pursue an evaluation.

Learning or social/behavioral concerns can fall anywhere on a continuum. For children who are struggling a great deal, it is often easier to know that an evaluation would be helpful. However, parents may still want to know from the psychologist what information will be gained from specific assessment measures. For students who are struggling with reading, math or writing and are below grade level academically, there is usually good reason to better understand the nature of the difficulty in order to provide targeted intervention to support learning. If parents are concerned about social or behavioral issues that may be interfering with school, family or peer relationships, they may be interested in obtaining an accurate assessment and finding out what interventions would allow the child to be more successful socially. There are also students who have complex needs and psychologists can help parents understand how the different elements of an evaluation can be helpful in putting the pieces together.

Students experiencing more subtle difficulties may be more puzzling for parents. Some students may be quite bright, even gifted, yet seem to struggle with reading or writing. Others seem to have strong academic skills, but the concern is related to focus, attention or other interfering behaviors. Some parents feel that their child is capable but seems unmotivated and are unsure if there is a learning issue that underlies the lack of motivation. Based on this initial discussion, the evaluator can help the parent know how an evaluation would help tease out these complex factors. This, in turn, often helps parents to make a decision about whether testing makes sense.

Parents who have had concerns about their child's development and academic progress may begin by speaking with their child's teacher. However, it is also reasonable to consult with other school-based professionals such as a school psychologist, learning specialist or principal. There are resources available in public school to address parental concerns. It is possible to call for an EMT (Educational Management Team) meeting which is held to evaluate parent or teacher concerns and to decide whether further assessment is indicated. Parents meet with a child's teacher(s), a school administrator, a learning specialist and often a school psychologist who as a team review progress and decide whether the concerns warrant an evaluation. If the team decides that an evaluation is indicated, they then plan for what specialists will be involved and what type of assessments will be completed.

This public school evaluation is free of charge. However, it is sometimes not as comprehensive or individualized as a private evaluation. It also may not be completed as quickly since there is often a lengthy process for determining the need for testing.

Some parents may prefer to consult with a private psychologist. They may be seeking a more in-depth evaluation than the public school might offer. Sometimes the public school team may not feel that an evaluation is warranted, but parents may want to pursue one anyway. Other parents like the fact that a private evaluation is more independent or they may want to have more control over choosing the psychologist who will conduct the evaluation. For students who attend private school, there is not always a psychologist on staff who can conduct an evaluation. These families typically also seek out private psychologists. Private evaluations can be more costly, although it is possible that some of the cost can be covered by insurance.

I'm ready to begin this process. What happens next?

If parents feel that they want to pursue an evaluation, the next step is for the evaluator to gather a full developmental history at an intake appointment. The initial intake meeting is a time for parents to become comfortable with the evaluator and with the testing process. Parents may come to the evaluation with certain fears or hesitancy about whether the evaluator will "get" their child. They may have questions about how their child will be made to feel comfortable. Parents sometimes have had family members who have made comments such as "it's just laziness" or "it's just bad parenting". However, after talking with a psychologist, parents may be reassured to hear that psychologists generally subscribe to the theory that students generally do well if they can do well. Psychologists are likely to consider that resistance to doing work or other behavioral issues may not be related to either laziness or bad parenting. A carefully done evaluation may clarify what the real issues are that contribute to the child's difficulty.

Why is the history important?

Gathering the history is important for a variety of reasons. First, it provides the evaluator with information about whether the presenting concerns are long-standing or more recent. Diagnostically, certain developmental concerns are characterized by a history that begins in early childhood. Other difficulties coincide with early academic instruction or can be transient or situational in nature. A second important reason for history gathering is that it provides the evaluator with a sense for the whole child and whether there are multiple factors at play. For example, a child may have a history of language delays as a preschooler, followed by delays in reading or writing which are evident in kindergarten and first grade. The interrelationship of factors and the developmental trajectory of these factors are important in conceptualizing the nature of the problem. A third reason for obtaining this history is to help the evaluator determine the specific tests and other assessment measures that may be useful in clarifying the nature of the concerns.

Preparing for the intake meeting

Parents can prepare for the intake meeting by thinking about all the questions they would like to have answered by the evaluation. This helps the evaluator to focus the evaluation and be sure that the measures chosen will provide insight into the questions or goals that parents have. The evaluator will likely explore these questions in detail to better understand the nature of the concerns and to think about how best to organize the evaluation.

There can be many different goals for an evaluation, such as:

- Evaluating why a student is struggling in a particular academic area such as reading
- Evaluating how attention weaknesses are impacting academic performance

- Assessing whether school-based anxiety is related to some type of learning weakness

- Providing admissions testing for private school

- Assessing cognitive abilities and academic skills to inform the Individualized Educational Program (IEP) process in public school

- Evaluating behavioral concerns in order to support development of social skills or improve behavioral regulation

- Determining what educational accommodations or supports would be helpful to a child in school

At the intake meeting, the evaluator will explore the presenting concerns, the developmental and educational history, the child's strengths and interests and other factors that may be related. Parents should identify questions they have based on their own concerns and those raised by teachers. The psychologist refines these questions and adds to them based on listening to the factual information, the developmental history and observations. In the end, the goal of the evaluation is to integrate the history and observations with the test data to make diagnostic conclusions and to plan for intervention and educational supports.

The following guide may be helpful in preparing for this meeting and knowing what to bring:

What might be asked?	What you should bring with you (if you have it).
What are the parent and/or teacher concerns?	You may want to make a list of your questions or concerns that teachers have mentioned.
Describe the child's personality, interests and strengths.	This information is usually gathered through discussion and helps the evaluator get a sense for the child including talents and strengths.

Think about the child's development of skills in language, visual processing, gross and fine motor skills, memory, and attention	If you have kept developmental records, bring them. Report cards are also helpful. Think about whether your child has ever participated in speech and language therapy, occupational therapy or was diagnosed with any weaknesses in these areas. If there were evaluations or progress reports written based on these services, it is useful to share them.
Discuss the child's progress with reading, math and writing	Report cards and school based standardized testing results can be helpful if you have them. If you have prior testing, provide it. If your child has participated in any kind of academic intervention in these areas, describe the nature of it and whether it was helpful.
How does the child do socially? Are there any issues with anxiety or depression or any behavioral concerns?	This is usually conveyed through discussion. If the child has been previously diagnosed or treated for any behavioral concerns, share that information.
Are there any health concerns or family history of learning or emotional problems?	Share any relevant health history or family history of similar learning or behavioral concerns.

How comprehensive an evaluation does my child need?

Psychoeducational evaluations can vary considerably in terms of the extent of the assessment process. Based on the referral concerns, the psychologist can advise parents about whether a briefer evaluation or a more comprehensive evaluation is appropriate. A relatively brief evaluation may involve a more behavioral assessment if the concerns are behavioral rather than academic. A brief educational evaluation may involve an IQ test and an achievement test to provide a basic profile of thinking abilities and academic skills in reading, writing and math. On the other hand, a full battery or comprehensive psychoeducational evaluation may involve many tests of cognitive abilities and academic skills, questionnaires and school observations.

There are situations where a brief evaluation may make sense. If the developmental history suggests that the diagnostic question is primarily related to Attention Deficit Hyperactivity Disorder (ADHD) or anxiety, and that cognitive and academic skills are quite strong in all areas, it is possible to do a behavioral evaluation without cognitive or academic testing. For concerns related to ADHD, this would involve reviewing the developmental history and current behaviors having to do with activity level, restlessness, impulsivity, distractibility and executive function skills, observing and/or interviewing the child and completing questionnaires having to do with attention and executive function skills. Other possible rule-outs may include evaluation of anxiety, depression, sleep issues and other health issues that may present similarly to ADHD.

This very circumscribed evaluation (without cognitive or academic testing) may help to diagnose ADHD and may be appropriate if someone is considering the use of medication for ADHD. However, there is a subgroup of individuals with ADHD who also have learning issues. Doing a purely behavioral evaluation may not catch students with related learning problems. In addition, if parents are seeking to obtain educational accommodations for their student with ADHD such as classroom support for attention, help with organization and executive function skills, or extra time for tests, it is necessary to demonstrate the educational impact of ADHD on academic performance. Being diagnosed with ADHD may not be sufficient in itself to qualify for educational accommodations without demonstrating how the child's attention weaknesses affect academic performance and classroom functioning. For these reasons, at least a brief evaluation including IQ and achievement testing may be useful.

If the primary concern is anxiety, sometimes clinicians may choose to limit the evaluation to a behavioral or emotional assessment. However, if parents feel that their child's anxiety is having an effect on academic performance, it may make sense to do at least a basic educational assessment. It is possible that the child's anxiety is interfering with academic performance. However, the converse may also be true, that some subtle academic weakness is contributing to school-based anxiety. In order to obtain accommodations for anxiety at school, it will be important to show how anxiety and academic performance are related.

A comprehensive evaluation is often a good choice if a student has academic weaknesses and it is not clear what is contributing to these difficulties. For example, parents may not be sure if a reading difficulty is related to weak language skills, weak decoding skills or weak attention skills. Parents may feel that there are a variety of factors impacting academic skills and may want a comprehensive assessment. Some parents are not sure if their child has both attention weaknesses and learning issues. Other parents have been puzzled for a while and want a complete evaluation of cognitive abilities, attention, academic skills and social/emotional factors to be sure that all factors are assessed. In these situations, a comprehensive evaluation is usually recommended to get at the full range of factors and to determine the impact of these factors on academic performance.

A comprehensive psychoeducational evaluation is likely to explore numerous aspects of cognitive processing (the thinking skills that underlie learning), including multiple dimensions of language processing and verbal reasoning, nonverbal reasoning and visual processing, memory skills, executive function skills, attention skills, and processing speed. In addition, this type of evaluation will likely use multiple measures which are more comprehensive in nature to provide more in-depth testing of reading, math and writing. For example, a comprehensive reading evaluation may include assessment of phonological awareness (sounding out words), fluency (reading speed), and comprehension under different conditions (timed reading, oral reading, silent reading, reading comprehension from memory or with the opportunity to refer back to the text). A comprehensive math evaluation may look at aspects of math reasoning and computation including strategy use for problem-solving, spatial skills related to math, math facts fluency, number sense, working memory and sequencing skills. A comprehensive writing evaluation might look at factors related to handwriting skills, ideation for writing, written output speed, organization of writing, language skills related to writing and writing mechanics (spelling, punctuation, and capitalization). Writing assessments may also include very structured sentence-writing prompts and more open-ended writing prompts, such as writing an essay. In addition, a comprehensive evaluation may explore other aspects related to learning, such as social/emotional factors and attention.

Developing a testing plan

After carefully gathering the history and listening to the presenting concerns, the psychologist will develop a testing plan. Because cognitive abilities are fundamentally related to academic achievement, clinicians test both cognitive abilities and specific academic skills. There are numerous tests that measure factors related to cognitive abilities, academic skills, attention/executive function skills, social/emotional factors, and fine motor skills for individuals of different ages. The psychologist will carefully choose assessments that are age appropriate and also specific to the referral questions. There are also a number of very useful questionnaires that may be chosen to gather observations and impressions from parents, teachers and from the child, if appropriate. These questionnaires provide observations from those who know the child best and from the child as well. In addition to these tests and questionnaires, the psychologist may suggest other ways of gathering relevant information such as a classroom observation or a play-based session. These choices help to answer questions that are hard to get at in the office or during formal testing. In this way, the psychologist builds an individualized testing plan by including elements that are specific to the presenting concerns and comprehensive enough to answer the diagnostic questions. A list of more commonly used tests and questionnaires is provided in the Appendix. Chapter 2 will provide information on how cognitive abilities and academic skills are related. Chapter 3 will describe different types of assessments that may be helpful. Parents should expect that the evaluator will describe the tests that will be administered and other sources of information that will be gathered, along with a rationale for why they have been chosen and what they measure.

What can I expect from the evaluation?

Some parents wonder whether a psychoeducational evaluation will be limited to diagnostic findings or whether the evaluator will provide recommendations and suggestions for intervention and supports. Psychologists vary in their familiarity with teaching and in their ability to translate test findings into recommendations for educational intervention. However, most parents would prefer an evaluation that provides diagnostic findings and also makes connections between the diagnostic information and educational intervention as well as interventions to address social/behavioral concerns. Good psychoeducational evaluations make explicit the relationships between cognitive abilities and academic skills, clarify the impact of social/behavioral issues or attention/executive function issues on learning and also make specific recommendations for supports and accommodations at school and outside of school.

Characteristics of a good psychoeducational evaluation

- It provides a comprehensive history, which includes the child's development in areas related to the evaluation questions.

- It provides information about a child's personality, interests, and strengths.

- It clarifies specific questions that should be answered by the evaluation.

- The tests chosen and other information gathered are relevant to the presenting concerns and will clarify specific factors related to these concerns.

- The evaluation is properly paced to the child's age and ability to work and provides support and incentives, if necessary, to address motivation and to maintain the child's engagement and interest.

- The results are communicated verbally and in writing in a manner that is easy to understand by parents, educators and other professionals.

- The report is written with its intended audience in mind. If the report is for a school setting, it should address areas that are relevant for the child's education.

- There is a diagnostic formulation that synthesizes the test findings and connects cognitive findings, social/behavioral findings, and attention issues, if relevant, to the educational findings.

- There are recommendations for next steps including supports, interventions, accommodations and possible medical referrals that would be helpful. Recommendations are specific to the test findings and are not boilerplate recommendations.

- If appropriate, parents are coached about using the report to ask for public school special education and/or accommodations, such as an IEP or a 504 plan or to seek alternative school placements.

CHAPTER 2

What is the relationship between cognitive abilities and academic skills?

Comprehensive evaluations assess both cognitive abilities and academic skills to understand the relationship between thinking skills and school performance. Cognitive abilities have to do with all of the thinking and processing abilities such as language skills, memory skills, visual processing, visual motor skills, attention and executive function skills. When presented with concerns about academic achievement, the goal is to find out what underlying cognitive processing abilities or challenges are contributing to academic difficulties. Increasingly, research has been able to study the relationship between academic skills and brain function (Feifer, 2013; Feifer, 2017; Feifer and DeFina, 2000; Goldberg, 2001; Hale and Fiorello, 2004). This research has begun to clarify how academic skills such as reading, math, and writing are processed in the brain. From this research, clinicians are better able to clarify this relationship, which is important both to the diagnostic process and to resultant intervention recommendations. For example, a reading difficulty can be related to difficulty with memory, phonics, attention, or language comprehension. As a result, for an individual student, it is important to make these connections diagnostically to identify the best approach for intervention.

The charts that follow provide a guide to how some aspects of cognitive processing may impact academic skills:

COGNITIVE PROCESSES RELATED TO READING

A cognitive weakness in...	may be seen in these difficulties with reading:
Attention and executive function skills	• Inconsistency in visual discrimination and letter reversals, transpositions of letter sequence, and omission of symbols when decoding because of weak attention • Processing of only one visual feature leading to incorrect association with sound • Impulsiveness resulting in a tendency to guess the entire word based on the first letter • Difficulty retaining the whole decoding process because of distractibility • Poor self-monitoring, which interferes with decoding when the child fails to ask, "Does this sound right?" • Difficulty working systematically at decoding in early reading

COGNITIVE PROCESSES RELATED TO READING

A cognitive weakness in...	may be seen in these difficulties with reading:
Visual Processing	• Impairment in recognition of words • Confusion over directionality or other spatial characteristics resulting in inaccurate registration in visual memory and delays in consolidation of a sight-word vocabulary • Delays in automatic word recognition impacting reading speed • Slower visual processing impacting reading speed
Language	• Difficulty using linguistic knowledge which interferes with encoding and retrieval of information • Difficulty integrating visual print with verbal associations • A poor sense of phonology and appreciation of the specific sound elements of language • Semantic deficiencies resulting in an impoverished vocabulary and trouble associating words with their meanings • Syntactic weaknesses resulting in poor understanding of word order, which contributes to confusion about the meanings of words, phrases, and sentences
Working memory	• Poor recall of overall passage details • Poor retention of phonemic elements while sounding out words • Slower development of automaticity with sight word recall

COGNITIVE PROCESSES RELATED TO MATH

A cognitive weakness in...	may be seen in these difficulties with reading:
Attention and executive function skills	• Poor error detection and self-monitoring • Poor comprehension and application of concepts • Poor appreciation of details • Weak ability to organize the steps in multistep procedures • Weak strategy-use for solving word problems
Visual-spatial skills	• Trouble arranging numbers in columns and computing with irregular columns • Problems with regrouping in subtraction, addition, multiplication or division • Difficulty calculating with fractions and mixed numbers • Problems with geometry • Trouble using visualization and mental imagery to support math reasoning • Weak spatial working memory impacting estimation skills
Language	• Trouble understanding and processing word problems • Trouble with advanced algebra and calculus • Difficulty translating verbal terms such as *half* and *same* into numbers • Trouble interpreting linguistic complexities (indirect statements, inverted sequence, too much information, semantic ambiguity, implicit information, important little words)

COGNITIVE PROCESSES RELATED TO MATH

A cognitive weakness in...	may be seen in these difficulties with reading:
Sequential ordering	• Difficulty following multistep explanations • Difficulty understanding time concepts • Difficulty solving problems that call for executing a sequential stepwise process or deconstructing numbers
Graphomotor skills	• Trouble transcribing legible numbers and arranging them on a page
Higher-order cognition and problem-solving	• Difficulty understanding math concepts at a deep level • Trouble getting started because of failure to extract key words or ideas that indicate the best strategy to use in solving problems • Difficulty with reorganizing a problem to simplify it for problem-solving • Difficulty engaging in extended chains of logical reasoning • Difficulty distinguishing relevant from irrelevant details
Working memory	• Trouble holding the elements of a problem in memory while solving it • Difficulty with efficient recall of math facts and procedures because of weaker rapid-retrieval memory

COGNITIVE PROCESSES RELATED TO WRITING

A cognitive weakness in......	may be seen in these difficulties with reading:
Attention and executive function skills	• Lack of self-monitoring and attention to fine detail • May do well on spelling tests when attention is focused on words in isolation, but spelling deteriorates when writing text • Difficulty with organization of ideas in writing • Difficulty simultaneously shifting attention from ideas to spelling, writing mechanics, organization or editing • Losing track of ideas while writing • Excessive time needed to create output • Simplistic sentence structure • Lack of capitalization, punctuation • Poor use of transitional words and elaboration of ideas • Poor self-monitoring while writing • Difficulty shifting attention from a white board to desktop tasks
Spatial and sequential ordering	• Weak skills make appreciation of the whole word harder • Poor sequential sound segmentation noted in difficulty writing multi-syllable words • Difficulty presenting information in a logical and organized manner to improve understanding by the reader

COGNITIVE PROCESSES RELATED TO WRITING

A cognitive weakness in......	may be seen in these difficulties with reading:
Memory	• Poor retrieval memory often noted in weak spelling and weak memory for spelling rules • Difficulty with recall of ideas or facts • Weak retrieval and rapid application of writing mechanics • Weak visual memory related to weak memory for appearance of letters, letter patterns, and words • Weakness in active working memory making it difficult to simultaneously remember ideas, how to spell, punctuation, and motor aspects of writing
Language	• Word-finding difficulty making it difficult to express ideas on paper • Weakness in oral syntax reflected in errors with written syntax • Difficulty with pragmatic language contributing to difficulty appreciating the needs and understanding of the audience • Limited vocabulary knowledge affecting understanding of word endings or prefixes • Difficulty with ideation for writing • Weak skills in phonological awareness leading to faulty spelling skills and a tendency to do minimalistic writing.

COGNITIVE PROCESSES RELATED TO WRITING

A cognitive weakness in......	may be seen in these difficulties with reading:
Higher-order cognition	• Weakness in logical writing and use of writing to present an argument • Writing lacking in sophistication of ideas, abstract language, and supportive details • Difficulty with reasoning and writing at the same time • Writing tends to be concrete without references or generalization • Written work tends to read like a list of unintegrated facts or details • Difficulty with demands to extrapolate, to make inferences, or to generalize in expression of ideas
Developmental-coordination disorder	• Difficulty writing letters accurately • Motor-planning difficulty can affect overall motor aspects of writing

Making the connection between cognitive and academic weaknesses helps direct intervention strategies. For some children with language weaknesses related to reading, intervention may focus on building language skills such as vocabulary, syntax, and skills in conceptualization to support reading comprehension. Students with attention and executive function skill weaknesses related to writing may benefit from using graphic organizers for writing or having the opportunity to talk through ideas orally with a teacher before starting to write. Students with memory weaknesses affecting math may be helped by strategies to gain automaticity with learning math facts or having examples of completed problems modeled visually at their desk. For some children, there may be multiple factors affecting reading, math or writing and clarifying these factors is helpful in educational planning for a particular child. This is why assessing both cognitive abilities and academic skills and understanding how the two are related are important diagnostically. Understanding this relationship is also helpful in targeting the best teaching practices for the individual child.

CHAPTER 3

What are the different types of tests and assessments that are typically used in a psychoeducational evaluation?

Based on the intake meeting and the presenting concerns, the evaluator will select tests and propose other ways of gathering relevant information to address the diagnostic questions that have been developed. These can include the following:

Parent, teacher, and self-report questionnaires

A variety of parent and teacher questionnaires are often used to gather information from individuals who see a child regularly. In addition, if it is age appropriate to do so, students may be asked to respond to self-report questionnaires. This information is helpful in making sure that the information gathered in the clinician's office is consistent with what parents and teachers see at home and school. Self-report questionnaires also give the evaluator a sense for the child's perspective. Most of these questionnaires are norm-referenced, which means that parent, teacher, and self-report ratings are compared with a sample of respondents across the country.

These ratings are often used to assess attention, executive function skills, social/emotional behaviors, and factors related to autism and adaptive skills. Evaluators may also give out questionnaires that are not norm-referenced, which ask a parent or teacher to rate a child on specific skills, often related to reading, writing, math or other aspects of development. These ratings are more descriptive in nature and help the evaluator focus the evaluation more precisely in areas of concern.

Tests that measure cognitive abilities

There are a wide variety of tests that measure cognitive abilities such as language skills, fine motor skills, spatial skills, visual processing, memory skills, nonverbal reasoning, attention and executive function skills. IQ tests measure cognitive abilities and are basic to most psychoeducational evaluations. They provide a way to estimate a child's overall abilities and pattern of cognitive strengths and weaknesses. The most commonly used IQ tests are the Wechsler tests which include the Wechsler Preschool and Primary Scale of Intelligence - Fourth Edition (WPPSI-IV), which is for children between the ages of 2 ½ and 7 ½, the Wechsler Intelligence Scale for Children - Fifth Edition (WISC-V), for children between the ages of 6 and 16, and the Wechsler Adult Intelligence Scale - Fourth Edition (WAIS-IV), which is for individuals age 16 and up. There are other IQ measures which include the Stanford-Binet - Fifth Edition (SB5), the Kaufman Assessment Battery for Children - Second Edition (KABC-II), and the Differential Abilities Scales - Second Edition (DAS-II). There are also nonverbal tests of intelligence, such as the Comprehensive Test of Nonverbal Intelligence - Second Edition (CTONI-2) and the Leiter International Performance Scale - Third Edition (Leiter-3). In addition to IQ measures, there are numerous tests of specific cognitive abilities, which may be chosen by an evaluator interested in in-depth assessment in a particular area. These tests typically measure cognitive abilities such as language, memory, fine motor skills, nonverbal-reasoning skills, spatial skills, attention and executive function skills. Each of these tests typically provides more comprehensive assessment in the area being evaluated than the more general assessment tools.

Tests that measure academic achievement

The most commonly used general achievement tests are the Woodcock Johnson IV Test of Achievement and the Wechsler Individual Achievement Test - Fourth Edition (WIAT-IV). These are general achievement tests, which measure skills in reading, written language and math. They are helpful in getting a sense for where a child is functioning relative to peers in the areas measured. There are also numerous single-subject tests of specific academic skills within reading, writing, and math. These tests are typically chosen in addition to a generalized achievement test to assess reading, math or writing skills using more in-depth measures or different formats to answer specific questions about academic concerns in these areas.

Tests of social/emotional factors

There are a variety of measures used to evaluate social and emotional factors. Projective testing is one method of understanding a child's emotional life. Projective testing is based on an assumption that children will project their emotions onto the ambiguous stimuli presented to them and this, in turn, allows the evaluator to learn more about their emotional life. Projective testing can include Rorschach testing or tests of projective storytelling such as the Roberts Apperception Test - Second Edition (Roberts-2). Rorschach testing uses ambiguous inkblots and asks children to describe what they see. These responses are analyzed using one of several standardized scoring protocols. This analysis provides insight into a child's personality and how the child processes emotions. Projective story telling typically involves showing a child picture prompts and asking the child to create stories based on these pictures. The stories created can provide information about how the child processes certain emotions, perceives certain situations, problem-solves emotional situations, and how the child can organize thoughts and emotions. There are also tests of social problem-solving which measure a child's ability to do tasks such as read nonverbal social cues, take the perspective of another person, do social problem-solving, make social inferences or generalize from a situation. Social/emotional issues are also assessed with sentence completion tests, drawing tests, questionnaire measures and clinical observations.

Adaptive behavior assessments

Adaptive behavior assessments are interview/questionnaire measures typically completed with a parent or teacher and are used to determine if a child has age appropriate skills needed to live safely and independently in the community. Typically, these measures involve gathering information about communication skills, daily-living or self-help skills, and social skills. These types of assessments are particularly relevant for students with significant developmental delays and are often required to make a determination about intellectual impairment and appropriate educational placements.

Computer-based tests of attention

Some clinicians use computer-based tests of attention such as the Test of Variables of Attention (T.O.V.A.), the Connors Continuous Performance Test - Second Edition (CPT-II), or the Integrated Visual and Auditory Continuous Performance Test - Second Edition (IVA-2 CPT). These tests require students to watch stimuli presented on a computer screen and respond by clicking a mouse when certain prompts appear. The child's responses are then evaluated for factors such as vigilance, distractibility and impulsivity. However, evaluation of ADHD should never be based on a computer-based test alone. Thorough assessment of ADHD should be based on gathering a careful developmental history, direct observation, questionnaire measures and these computer-based tests, if indicated.

Classroom observation measures

Observing in the classroom provides an opportunity to get a sense for how the child responds within that environment and to the task demands presented there. Many of these variables are not evident in the evaluator's office, but may be important in diagnosis and in making recommendations for intervention. Factors that may be observed in the classroom include the teacher-student ratio, the level of stimulation and structure in the class, the curriculum demands, the child's ability to manage what is presented in the classroom, the level of support given to the student, the child's attention, engagement, etc. Since the observer is typically in the classroom for a relatively short amount of time, it is important that the evaluator chooses a period of time to observe that provides the opportunity to watch different types of activities, such as a teacher-directed activity, independent work time, activities that involve social interaction with peers (if relevant), and possibly recess, depending on the presenting concerns. When setting up a school observation, it is particularly important to ask the child's teacher what the best times are to observe the classroom activities that will provide insight into the specific diagnostic questions. Sometimes these observations are completed before the child has met the evaluator, so that the child is not aware that they are being observed.

Functional Behavior Assessments (FBAs)

A functional behavior assessment (FBA) is a way of assessing problem behaviors that interfere with a child's functioning in the school setting. Parental permission is necessary for the school to conduct an FBA. After this permission is given, a behavior specialist (who may be a psychologist) collects information to determine the nature of the behavior in order to develop a plan to modify it. This person observes where and when the behavior occurs, noting its frequency, duration, intensity, rate, and location. The observer notes what was happening before the behavior began, what the problem behavior looked like, and what reaction the student received in the environment. From the data gathered, the evaluator makes hypotheses about what is triggering that behavior and whether it is motivated by frustration, a desire to avoid an activity, a desire for attention or other factors. The evaluator may also take note of what interventions are currently being used, what interventions have been used in the past, and what has or has not been successful in modifying the behavior. Proposed intervention strategies derived from an FBA can focus on averting the behavior, reacting differently to it, or adapting the classroom to improve the child's ability to be successful._

CHAPTER 4

What information can be best gathered from a classroom observation?

The classroom provides many opportunities to obtain information about variables that are not easily observed in the one-to-one setting of the examiner's office. To the degree that the classroom differs from the office and because a great deal of the student's time is spent in the classroom, these variables are relevant to understanding the student's experience.

In some ways, the examiner's office may provide an optimized setting in which to evaluate a student's abilities. It is typically one-on-one, quiet, less stimulating, and less distracting than the classroom. The examiner is present to explain, repeat (if permitted) and direct attention, which is typically quite different from performing in the classroom with its intrinsic distractions. In this sense, the evaluator's office may in some ways optimize the student's typical performance. On the other hand, the office setting is likely new and unfamiliar to the child. The examiner is a stranger. There are no familiar routines, no teacher who has already established rapport, nor a physical setting which has become familiar. For those reasons, it is incumbent on the evaluator both to establish rapport in the office and to observe at school to get a good sense of the child in both environments.

The classroom is also a particularly important setting to evaluate attention, engagement, social skills with peers and interactions with adults. The examiner may attempt to obtain this information from parent and teacher questionnaires, but observing directly in the classroom provides the evaluator with important first-hand clinical data as well.

In addition, the classroom-based curriculum is often different from the testing tasks and may be more complex or involve cognitive skills that are not easily assessed with formal testing. This is because the curriculum varies in different schools. It evolves and changes more rapidly than standardized achievement testing does. In addition, by its nature, standardized testing must be appropriate for students across the country, who make up the normative group used for test development, but who are exposed to a variety of curricula or teaching approaches.

An example of this difference can be observed in the area of math. The calculation portion of an achievement test may involve testing a student's knowledge of math algorithms at different grade levels. Two-digit by two-digit multiplication on the test is presented in a traditional format with two digits under another two digits vertically. However, the curriculum at school may not require children to do two-digit multiplication in this format. At school, the student may be asked to deconstruct the two-digit number into tens and ones or estimate based on the tens column before adding. The observer may also find that in the classroom, the student is required to demonstrate two or three different ways of finding the answer to this problem. For some students who struggle with math, it is this aspect of the curriculum that causes difficulty, and this is not measured in a standard math achievement test. In addition, at many schools, the classroom math work may involve writing a paragraph about how the student arrived at the answer. This math task is also a writing task and requires good writing skills in addition to math skills. Writing one's ideas about math is not tapped by standardized math achievement tests. If the examiner is interested in finding out how a student's cognitive strengths and weaknesses impact academic performance, assessing these classroom-based variables is key to a more accurate and relevant evaluation.

When doing a classroom observation, these are some variables the evaluator may consider:

Classroom structural variables

- How many students are in the class?
- How many teachers, assistant teachers, specialists are in the classroom?
- How are the students organized (e.g., at individual desks, sitting in groups, working on the floor)?
- How long are the instructional periods (e.g., twenty minutes of whole group instruction followed by independent work)?
- Are there opportunities for movement between activities?
- How is the need for extra support addressed in the classroom?
- Are there opportunities for individual/small group instruction?
- Is the classroom programming structured or more free-flowing?

Attention and executive-function skills

- What is the child's activity level and ability to focus? Does it change based on the subject matter?
- Is the child impulsive with respect to response style when doing work or responding to questions in the classroom? Is the child impulsive with peers in a social sense?
- Is the child easily distracted while doing tasks?

- How able is the child to get started with tasks in the classroom without individualized support?

- Can the child hold a set of instructions or procedures in mind while working?

- How able is the child to plan out an assignment and to carry out the steps needed to complete it?

- Does the child know how to check their work for mistakes?

- How able is the child to take note of assignments and to organize materials?

Social/emotional factors

- How readily does the child engage with activities?

- How motivated is the child to work?

- How able is the child to engage with peers in large and small group interactions?

- How flexible is the child in adapting to changes in routines and transitions in the classroom?

- Is there evidence of anxiety or other mood-related issues?

- Are there situations where the child seems to get stuck?

- How able is the child to self-regulate behaviorally?

- How does the child cope with frustration in the learning process or socially?

- Does the child have age appropriate social skills with peers?

Task demands

- How are instructions given?
  - Orally to the whole class

- ○ Orally, followed by individual review of instructions

- ○ Checklists at the student's desk

- ○ Written on the board

- ○ Universal design (providing instruction in multiple modalities to allow students to process the instructions in a manner that best suits them)

- Are the task demands at the level of the child's abilities?

- How does the student respond when stuck?

- How does the child react to starting and stopping activities?

- What is required as output?

  - ○ Responding orally

  - ○ Responding in writing

  - ○ Drawing or a creating something

- What supports are provided if the student needs extra help?

Identifying the breakdown point with specific task demands

For students who are having difficulty with specific aspects of the curriculum, it is often useful to try to identify where the breakdown point is in complex academic tasks. The breakdown point is where the child becomes stuck or where the skills necessary to do the task are not yet acquired by the student. In order to do this, the observer needs to have a sense of the task as a whole, the sequence of steps that make up the task, and the cognitive abilities or academic skills that are required to do the task competently. Based on this analysis, the evaluator can develop a plan for systematically teaching the subskills necessary to perform the task.

Consider the following examples of skills involved in writing a research paper, responding to reading comprehension questions or solving a word problem in math.

Skills involved in writing a research paper

- Coming up with an idea (if not provided by the assignment)

- Breaking the larger task into a sequence of steps

- Deciding what information needs to be researched

- Finding sources

- Taking notes about the information found

- Organizing the paper

- Handwriting, dictating, or typing the paper

- Sequencing the ideas into paragraphs

- Editing the paper for spelling, punctuation, and grammar

- Estimating the amount of time needed to complete the task

- Working day by day toward the end goal

Skills involved in responding to reading comprehension questions

- Being able to decode the reading material

- Processing the language of the text

- Understanding the vocabulary

- Recalling the material

- Being able to generalize, draw inferences or do critical analysis of text

- If the response required is in written form, being able to do the written output either by drawing, handwriting, dictating, or typing

- Having skills in spelling, punctuation, capitalization and editing to create well-written sentences.

Skills involved in solving a word problem in math

- Understanding the language of the word problem

- Differentiating essential from non-essential information to solve the problem

- Being able to break the problem apart and determine the sequence of steps necessary to solve the problem

- Knowing the math algorithms that are relevant to the problem

- Knowing math facts by heart

- Organizing the problem spatially on the page

- Doing the written output required

- Maintaining attention throughout the problem without becoming distracted when sequencing the steps in the problem solving process

For each of these academic tasks, the evaluator can identify where the breakdown point happens for an individual student. Sometimes formal testing may provide information about this, but it is also often useful to observe in the classroom, to analyze work samples, or to work with the child during the office-based assessment to understand where in the process the child has difficulty. Teachers, parents, and tutors can be helpful in gathering this information. Older students sometimes are aware of where they have difficulty and can identify breakdown points if asked. The evaluator may also do an informal assessment, which parallels a school-based academic task to get at these aspects of academic concerns.

Learner-centered evaluation

Another approach to the assessment process is to start with a learner-centered focus and assess what a learner understands are their strengths, challenges, preferences, and needs when learning. In their book, *How to Personalize Learning* (2017), Barbara Bray and Kathleen McClaskey have developed an approach to personalized learning that can be adapted to the psychoeducational evaluation process. This approach is built upon the concept of Universal Design for Learning (UDL). UDL is a set of principles for curriculum development to allow all students to have the opportunity to learn by creating educational goals, methods, materials, and assessments that work for diverse learners. UDL principles and guidelines include providing multiple means of engagement (options for engaging with learning), multiple means of representation (options for accessing and processing of material), and multiple means of action and expression (options for expressing what you know and understand). Bray and McClaskey use the terms *access*, *engage*, and *express* as a practical way of applying these UDL principles. The premise behind their approach is a belief that for learners to ultimately be successful in school and post-school, they need to be aware of their strengths, challenges, preferences, and needs regarding how they learn. This awareness allows them to know who they are as learners and develop the skills to support their learning that would result in being a self-directed learner. The belief is that when students develop agency in their own learning, it increases motivation, self-direction, and self-advocacy in their learning process.

The three-step process that Bray and McClaskey advocate for teachers to use also has an application for the psychoeducational evaluation process and has the potential to provide important information that is not typically gathered as part of traditional assessment. In addition to gaining diagnostic information that is important in developing educational plans, the process is also an intervention in itself to help students become more invested in their own learning.

This approach is appropriate for students in later elementary, middle, and high school. The process involves first asking students about who they are (interests, talents, passions and aspirations). Next, using the UDL Lens of Access, Engage and Express™, students would share their strengths, challenges, preferences, and needs in how they access new information, engage with content and concepts, and express what they know and understand. This information can involve responding to a questionnaire or survey where the students choose from a list of strengths and challenges, selecting those that they believe apply to them in these three domains (access, engagement, and expression), followed by talking with students about their strengths and challenges in their learning. The learner is also asked in this conversation to share preferences or needs for supports and strategies for learning, including the use of tools, apps, learning skills, and strategies that would be part of their Personal Learning Backpack™. The students are also asked about their interests, talents, passions, and aspirations to understand the affective side of their learning. The information can be summarized in what Bray and McClaskey call the Learner Profile™ and the Personal Learning Backpack™ template, an example of which is shown here:

Name:				Date:
Learner Profile				**Personal Learning Backpack**
	Strengths	**Challenges**	**Preferences and Needs**	**Tools, Apps, Resources; Learning Strategies/Skills**
Access	• I can visualize what I hear. • I connect to ideas I already know.	• I often do not understand what I read. • I have trouble focusing.	• I need to use a text-to-speech tool for reading. • I prefer to use video for understanding.	I would like to explore audio/text-to-speech for reading and comprehension as well as font options and access to my learning materials in digital format to use on my laptop/tablet, etc.
Engage	• I like to lead others. • I work well with others.	• I don't like doing difficult tasks.	• I need tasks to be broken down into smaller tasks. • I prefer to work with a partner.	I like working with a peer who knows how to help me break down tasks on projects. I like having a video that provides step-by-step instructions on developing new skills. I like a picture schedule or calendar with reminders that can help me to organize and stay on task.
Express	• I draw well. • I like telling stories orally. • I am a good presenter and speaker.	• I have trouble putting thoughts to paper. • I find note taking is difficult.	• I need to use a note taking tool. • I prefer graphic organizers to help me organize ideas. • I prefer to present orally.	I would like to use an audio recording app/technology to help me take notes and listen at the same time. I would like an app to help me brainstorm and organize ideas for writing. I would like to use multimedia where I can present information with audio, video, and/or drawings. I would like to be independent with finding mistakes and editing using word prediction or speech-to-text technology.
Words about me: Curious, Imaginative, Independent, Artistic, Friendly, Optimistic				
Interests, talents, and passions: Interested in soccer, baseball, and history. I am talented in storytelling, interpersonal skills, drawing, connecting the dots, and mental math. I am passionate about fishing and having my own business one day that helps people.				

Source: Copyright Bray & McClaskey 2017. How to Personalize Learning, Chapter 4, p.70. Used with Permission. Learner Profile, Personal Learning Backpack, and the UDL Lens of Access, Engage and Express are trademarks of Kathleen McClaskey. All rights reserved.

This process can be used along with traditional psychoeducational testing to create personalized goals for learning that acknowledge a student's strengths and goals as well as learning challenges. This information can also guide the creation of preferred supports to develop a personalized learning plan. For some students, particularly at the high school level, this approach has been used to help students develop their own plans for learning and for post-high school transition planning.

CHAPTER 5

How can the testing process be adapted to the needs of my child?

Standardized testing is based on specified administration of items within subtests and standardized rules for scoring. Every test manual provides instructions for how to administer the test, whether repetition of questions is allowed or not, whether examples are modeled or not, etc. Objective criteria for scoring are also provided. Standardized administration and scoring criteria contribute to the validity and reliability of the test. Deviating from standardized administration must always be described when reporting the test results so that the reader of the report knows that standard administration was adapted.

That said, it is sometimes very useful diagnostically to make some adaptations to standardized testing (which need to be described in the test report) or to do some trial teaching subsequent to standardized administration to clarify what supports are beneficial for a particular student. There are also some children who do not respond well to testing without adaptations. In these situations, making adaptations allows the evaluator to gain useful information and to make important diagnostic conclusions and educational recommendations that would otherwise not be feasible.

Certain adaptations, although not standardized, do not substantially compromise the validity of a test. These include:

- **Pacing of the evaluation sessions:** The most basic adaptation is to pace the evaluation appropriately for the child. Although some evaluators and some testing centers work with students for many hours or a whole day in one session, this can be very tiring for the student. Consideration should be given to the child's age, ability to focus and work for a particular length of time, and other factors that might help the student be comfortable and demonstrate skills. Parents are usually quite accurate in estimating how long their child can work in one session. Given the total amount of time estimated to complete the assessments, the clinician can suggest an appropriate pacing of sessions. For younger children, forty-five minutes to an hour may be appropriate. For this reason, a number of sessions may need to be scheduled. For high school students, two or three hours at a time may be reasonable. It is important never to continue with testing when a child is clearly unfocused, tired, not feeling well, or unmotivated, since the results are less likely to be valid.

- **Having the parent sit in on the evaluation:** Parents usually do not sit in with children during the assessment and doing so is typically discouraged. However, having the parent in the room is sometimes necessary with very young children or with elementary school students who are very anxious about separating from the parent. In this case, parental presence provides emotional support and may be the only way to accomplish the evaluation. The parent may sit in the room but preferably away from the evaluator and child, which allows standardized administration of tests. The only caveat or risk to this adaptation is that it may compromise the integrity of the test if the parent takes notes of items, shares them with others, or coaches their child deliberately or inadvertently. Parents should be counseled not to prompt the child, record anything about the evaluation questions, or in any way interfere with the testing process.

- **Having a tutor or an ABA therapist sit in on the evaluation**: This adaptation can be used to provide a familiar structure, motivators or reinforcement in a manner that is familiar to the child. For children who typically use a visual schedule for work periods, the testing subtests can be used to create a visual schedule. The child may be used to working in a particular way with the therapist who in turn uses the subtests of the test, which are administered in a standardized manner, to create a visual schedule and provide a schedule of reinforcements in a way that is typical of their work. The tutor or therapist will need to be provided with guidance about what is appropriate to say and what type of support is allowed. This person will often sit at the table with the evaluator. However, the evaluator administers the tests in a standardized manner and the involvement of a tutor or therapist is noted in the final report.

- **Using incentives during the evaluation**: Incentives such as small prizes, treats, or breaks to use a favorite toy may be used at whatever interval is necessary to improve focus and motivation. The test administration is conducted in a standardized manner, but the evaluator uses incentives throughout the evaluation at regular intervals to improve motivation.

Adaptations that are standardized:

- **Specialized testing**: The WISC-V Integrated is an example of a standardized test that provides adaptations to gain information about how the child processes information. The standard subtests from the WISC-V are used, but students do not have to generate as much language or respond with complex motor skills in

41

response to the subtest demands. As an example, on the vocabulary subtest, students are not required to define words in an open-ended manner but instead choose from multiple-choice options. With block design, students do not have to construct the designs with blocks but instead are asked to recognize a correctly formed design. This test is fully standardized and provides options for testing cognitive abilities with different formatting of tasks.

- **Tests of nonverbal intelligence**: There are tests of nonverbal intelligence which may be appropriate for estimating reasoning ability for students with language weaknesses, motor skill weaknesses, hearing impairment, or who are non-native English speakers. These tests are more visual in nature. Items are demonstrated visually and individuals can respond by pointing or by eye gaze, if necessary.

- **Creating a cascade of testing formats**: George McCloskey (2009) recommends using a series of standardized tests to create a *cascade* of formats that clarify the nature of a learning problem. For example, in order to evaluate executive function skills related to writing, the examiner might want to first use a test that is very structured and involves writing simple sentences, then use a test that involves more complex writing, such as synthesizing sentences, then have the student write an essay, which is completely open-ended. Each test is standardized, but the use of a series of tests, which increase in the complexity of the task, allows the examiner to make important statements about how the student works, where the breakdown occurs, and what strategies would be helpful.

Non-standardized adaptations to testing:

- **Trial teaching:** After administering and scoring a task from a test in a standardized manner, the evaluator may then attempt to see whether certain adaptations are useful to a student by trying the same task in a different format. For example, the standard task may be to write an open-ended essay with no support. After the student completes the essay in a standard way, the examiner may want to try to have the student do another essay (new topic) with a graphic organizer. Another example might be if a student was having difficulty with spatial aspects of math computation, the examiner might, after doing the regular math computation subtest, provide the student with graph paper and attempt similar problems. A third example might be if a student is having difficulty with strategy-use for math problem-solving, the evaluator might try some problems using some supports for breaking down a word problem. This is a way for the examiner to gain knowledge about what accommodations or teaching strategies may be effective based on the test findings. Scores are reported from standardized administration of the test items, but the evaluator can then speak to the benefit of certain task adaptations.

- **Foreign language adaptations:** Valid testing assumes that a student is a fluent English speaker. For children who are not native speakers of English, there are some standardized foreign language versions of tests. For example, there is a Spanish version of the WISC-V that is standardized. However, informally, it may make sense for a psychologist who speaks the child's native language to ask questions in that language to see whether the child is more competent in their native language and to establish which is the child's primary language. That said, it is not appropriate for the evaluator to translate standardized tests into other languages, since this invalidates the test.

CHAPTER 6

What do all these test scores and technical terms mean?

For parents who are not familiar with test scores, terms such as *standard scores, percentiles, grade equivalents, T scores and age/grade equivalents* presented in a report may be confusing. However, with an overview of these terms, parents will be much more able to interpret the evaluation findings. Most of these scores indicate how the child compares with others of the same age or grade with respect to the abilities or skills measured. Tests that are norm-referenced involve sampling a large group of children across the country. The scores that are derived provide a way to see how the child being tested compares to this normative sample with respect to their abilities to do the tasks being measured. These are some terms that are useful to understand:_

Standard scores: A standard score is a way of comparing a student to peers. It tells you how far a student is from average. Standard scores on tests are based on the average of children of the same age within the standardization sample of students across the country. Standard scores which are normally distributed form a bell curve, with most individuals scoring toward the middle and fewer individuals scoring at the extremes. A standard score is defined by its mean or average score and its standard deviation. The mean indicates what the average score is. The standard deviation tells you the degree to which scores typically deviate from average. Many cognitive and academic tests have a mean of 100 and a standard deviation of 15. If the average range is defined as one standard deviation above or below the mean, the average range may be defined as a standard score between 85 and 115.

Scaled scores: Some tests report individual subtest scores as scaled scores, which range from 1 to 19. Scaled scores also provide a way to compare a student to peers. A scaled score between 8 and 12 indicates that the child scored in the average range. Scores ranging from 13 to 19 reflect scores that are increasingly above average, and scores ranging from 7 to 1 represent scores that are increasingly below average.

Index score: Many tests group a set of subtests and provide an index score. This is a composite score typically for a set of subtests measuring one cognitive ability or academic skill (e.g., language skills or reading skills).

Raw scores: Raw scores are the number of correct answers on a test or subtest. The raw score does not indicate how the child is performing relative to peers. Without accounting for the child's age, raw scores often are not very meaningful. For this reason, raw scores are typically not provided in the test report.

T scores: T scores are another way of comparing a student to peers. A T score has a mean of 50 and a standard deviation of +/-10. One standard deviation above or below the mean (scores between 40 and 60) may characterize the average range. Scores above 60 would indicate above average scores and scores below 40 would indicate below average scores. It is important to take note of whether what is being measured is desirable or not. For example, an above average score on a measure of aggressiveness would indicate a negative attribute, whereas an above average score for social skills would indicate a positive attribute.

Percentile: The percentile tells you the percentage of scores that fall at or below a particular score. Percentile scores range from 1 to 99. For example, if a student's score is at the 60th percentile, that means that the student earned a score that is better than 60% of students taking this test. Percentiles are different from percentages. Percentages indicate the proportion of items that were answered correctly. For example, a student could earn 75% on a classroom test, which means that the student correctly answered 75% of the questions. However, a percentile score of 75 would indicate that the student's score was better than 75% of the students who took the test.

Confidence interval: The confidence interval is an estimate of the error of an individual's score due to the imperfect reliability of a test based on measurement procedure. If the 95% confidence interval of a score of 100 is +/-5, that means that 95% of the time, a child's true score is between 95 and 105.

Many tests also use qualitative descriptors to characterize scores within certain ranges. For example, the WISC-V uses the following descriptors to characterize IQ scores:

Extremely high	130 or above
Very high	120–129
High average	110–119
Average	90–109
Low average	80-89
Very low	70–79
Extremely low	below 70

The following chart provides a visual representation of terms related to standard scores, scaled scores, T scores, and percentile ranks, and possible descriptors for normally distributed scores.

Standard Scores

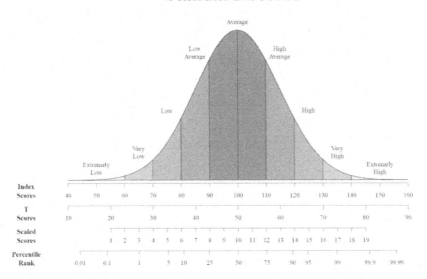

Retrieved from https://www.assessingpsyche.wordpress.com/category/psychometrics/page/2/

Age- and grade-equivalent scores: An age-equivalent (AE) score is a way of expressing the child's score in terms of what a typical or average student would earn at that age level. Age-equivalent scores are reported as years and months (AE: 8-4 means 8 years, 4 months). Grade-equivalent (GE) scores indicate how a child's score on a test compares to the average score obtained by a student at that grade level. These scores are reported as grade level and month (GE: 7.6 means grade 7, 6th month). Age- and grade-equivalent scores should be interpreted with caution and do not indicate that a child should be placed in that grade or with children of that age. These scores more accurately indicate that the child is above or below average when compared with students at their current age or grade.

Is the scoring of tests subjective?

Parents sometimes wonder if the scoring of tests is subjective. The development of norm-referenced and standardized tests is based on certain requirements. The test must establish a level of validity, that is, how well the test measures what it is supposed to be measuring. For example, if a test is supposed to be measuring reading fluency, its validity is a measure of how well it measures that dimension of the reading process. The test must also establish its reliability. Test-retest reliability has to do with how consistent the test scores would be if the child were to be assessed again with the same or similar version of the test. Inter-rater reliability measures how consistent the scores would be between different evaluators using the same test with the same child. The test developers must also provide strict guidance on the scoring of the student's responses. As a result, scoring of standardized tests is not subjective, and it is the objective scoring of the test that insures its validity and reliability.

CHAPTER 7

What should a good test report look like?

Reports from psychological evaluations can vary in the format used to communicate the evaluation findings. Typically, there is a section that provides information about the reason for referral and referral concerns. There is then a section that describes the background information or developmental history. This section should include early developmental milestones, development of cognitive abilities in the areas of language, visual processing, gross and fine motor skills, attention, memory, and social/emotional factors, as well as educational history of progress with reading, writing and math. Relevant medical issues and use of medication should also be discussed. Summarizing prior evaluations and school-based supports that have been provided is also important as part of the history. Often there is a section which describes the tests and procedures that have been used in the assessment process. The report then typically includes a section about behavioral observations during the assessment. In this section, the evaluator may comment about the child's engagement, rapport, attention, task persistence, language, approach to testing tasks, frustration tolerance, effort, and may include examples of observations noted during specific tasks.

Some reports provide a summary section at the beginning of report followed by specific test data. Other evaluators report findings from specific tests and then provide a summary and clinical formulation at the end of the report. Wherever this summary section is found, it should include diagnoses if appropriate, a synthesis of the evaluation findings, and how results are related to the presenting questions. Typically, after the diagnostic formulation and discussion of test results, there is a section which makes recommendations for school-based interventions and supports, accommodations in the classroom, and out-of-school interventions, such as tutoring, speech therapy, occupational therapy, specialized reading intervention, math intervention, writing intervention, or other supports such as psychotherapy or medical intervention.

Is there a way to make test findings more understandable and useful for teachers and parents?

Once the evaluation findings have been discussed, the next important task is to work toward implementing the findings and recommendations. Typically, a comprehensive psychoeducational report is quite lengthy and detailed. Sometimes it is not shared in its entirety with teachers and teachers may find the report to be too long, too detailed, or not tailored enough to their needs or to the teaching/learning process. Parents have the opportunity for a feedback meeting with the evaluator where the evaluation findings are discussed. However, parents often also feel the need to have results presented in a format that will be understandable and useful to them and to their child's teacher. The evaluation has the potential to offer a great deal to teachers but often needs some jargon and data translation both for parents and teachers.

What would parents and teachers like to see in this regard? The following summary chart is an example of how test findings can be presented in a format that may be more useful to readers.

SUMMARY OF TEST FINDINGS AND EDUCATIONAL RECOMMENDATIONS FOR STEVEN

TEST FINDINGS	LIKELY TO BE SEEN IN THE CLASSROOM AS:	RECOMMENDED EDUCATIONAL SUPPORT
Wechsler Intelligence Scale for Children – Fifth Edition (WISC-V) Verbal comprehension 87 Perceptual reasoning 84 Working memory 80 Processing speed 83 Full scale 79 Strengths: Better, age-appropriate skills with tasks that are more structured, with less complex executive-function demands for open-ended language organization or independent use of strategies Weaknesses: Tasks which involve fluid reasoning, i.e. novel problem-solving, flexible use of thinking skills; working memory, fine-motor speed affecting speed of written output. **Beery Developmental Test of Visual Motor Integration (VMI)** Test of Visual Motor Integration 87 Test of Visual Perception 114 Test of Visual-Motor Coordination 100 Low average skills in drawing designs. Above average skills in visual-perception and age-appropriate skills in fine-motor control (not speed)	• Likes school. • Responsive to praise and positive feedback. • Below average processing of verbal information affecting his processing of instruction and verbal directions, as well as his reading comprehension. • Below average skills in expressive language formulation. • Variable attention skills that need monitoring throughout the day. Academic skills can vary significantly depending on attention. • Needs demonstration of procedures and examples of how to do work provided in written form before beginning work independently. This reduces frustration and improves motivation. • Eager to do work that is familiar and understood. • Good decoding skills, sight-word recognition, and knowledge of phonics. • Difficulty with holding directions in mind while working independently.	**OVERALL TEACHING STRATEGIES:** • Be aware of marked weaknesses in language processing, which require simplification, review of concepts, support for language formulation, supplementation of directions with visual examples. • Be aware of a tendency to become overloaded, which, in turn, may be noted in behavioral issues, upset, or resistance to working. Provide breaks, simplification of tasks and opportunity to shift gears throughout the school day. • Be aware of the intrusiveness of extraneous thoughts about areas of interest and work to help him lay these thoughts aside. • Be aware of weaknesses in social reasoning that may affect his ability to answer certain questions. • Be more explicit throughout the day in helping him with strategy use in problem-solving. **SUPPORT FOR ATTENTION:** • Provide frequent breaks during the day. • Provide more frequent feedback during the day, particularly during independent work time. • Redirect him when he is over-focused on topics of interest that are distracting him from the task at hand. • Provide help for getting started with tasks, using modeling, examples, and beginning steps of a new task.

TEST FINDINGS	LIKELY TO BE SEEN IN THE CLASSROOM AS:	RECOMMENDED EDUCATIONAL SUPPORT
Wechsler Individual Achievement Test – Third Edition (WIAT-II) **ORAL LANGUAGE** 86 Listening comprehension 85 Receptive vocabulary 99 Oral discourse comprehension 76 Oral expression 86 Expressive vocabulary 107 Oral word fluency 83 Sentence repetition 88 **TOTAL READING** 106 **BASIC READING** 107 Reading comprehension and fluency 105 Early reading skills 101 Reading comprehension 105 Word reading 106 Pseudoword decoding 110 **ORAL READING FLUENCY** 103 Oral reading accuracy 105 Oral reading rate 102 **WRITTEN EXPRESSION** 86 Alphabet writing fluency 76 Spelling 95 Sentence composition 96 Sentence building 90 Sentence combining 104 **MATHEMATICS** 87 Math problem-solving 87 Numerical operations 89 **TOTAL ACHIEVEMENT** 92	• Difficulty with novel problem-solving tasks, tasks with complex executive-function demands or tasks that call for cognitive flexibility. • Slower written output. • Strong (obsessive) interest in cars and video games which intrudes on his thinking and distracts him. Over-focus on things of interest to him. • Weakness in social reasoning that impacts peer interaction and reading comprehension. • Good reading comprehension for factual information in text. • Reading-comprehension skills weaker with questions that call for drawing inferences, abstracting, predicting, and hypothesizing. • Open-ended writing negatively impacted by weaker expressive language formulation skills, weaker ideational skills, weaker organizational skills, executive function skills, slower written output speed, intrusion of irrelevant thoughts, and attention weaknesses. • Benefits from repetition in math and doing many problems of similar type and format. • Comprehension of new math procedures affected by weak working-memory skills, weaker language-processing skills, difficulty with novel problem-solving, and weaker attention.	• Provide checklists at his desk that he can check off to support self-monitoring while working. **SUPPORT FOR READING COMPREHENSION:** • When questions call for drawing inferences, provide more explicit clues on where to find information that addresses these questions. • Provide explicit support for social reasoning weaknesses in picking up on nonverbal clues or details that can be used to draw conclusions about inferential questions. • Provide questions ahead of time before he reads that will help him to look for clues to answer these more inferential questions. • Provide graphic organizers while reading to help him identify salient information to later answer inferential questions. • Practice drawing inferences in real life and in reading. • Provide much more individualized help with more abstract reading comprehensions calling for finding the main idea and predicting from the text. **SUPPORT FOR MATH:** • Provide a list of steps to do complex math computation that guides him with the appropriate procedural strategy. He can refer to his list (support for working memory) and can cross off the steps as he completes them (support for executive-function skills). • Practice with similar problem types, formatted similarly before introducing other formats.

TEST FINDINGS	LIKELY TO BE SEEN IN THE CLASSROOM AS:	RECOMMENDED EDUCATIONAL SUPPORT
Gray Oral Reading Test – Fourth Edition Rate 9 Accuracy 10 Fluency 10 Comprehension 8 Notes: Age-appropriate scores in reading fluency. Good sight-word recognition and phonics knowledge. Comprehension skills for factual information consistently good, but consistent difficulty with questions that call for drawing inferences, abstracting from text, hypothesizing, and social reasoning.	• Weaker retention for math skills when not reviewed regularly. • Behavior affected by level of frustration and confusion he experiences. Resistance to work is a cue that work needs to be explained differently, modeled for him, or broken down to make it more understandable. • Difficulty independently figuring out what strategy to use in novel problem-solving. • Difficulty with working memory impacts self-monitoring. Benefits from a written rubric to check off as he works.	• Review math procedures at intervals to support retention. • Provide visual supports for complex word problems as a support to weaker language-processing skills. • Practice learning math facts as a way to reduce working memory load and as a way to transition from counting real objects to automatic sight-word recognition of math facts. SUPPORT FOR WRITING: • Practice developing writing fluency by doing writing without any other demands for generating ideas, spelling, punctuation and organization. Just copying sentences would be an example. • Providing help with generating ideas for open-ended writing. He may need verbal discussion prior to writing. • He is likely to benefit from graphic organizers to help him organize ideas for writing. • When he is confused, reduce working memory demands in writing by separating idea generation as one step, sequencing ideas as a second step, then focusing on punctuation, and spelling as a third step. • Use scribing to reduce complex executive-function demands in writing. • Understand how difficulty with language, social inferencing, and expressive-language formulation impact writing, and provide support for each of these as needed in any given assignment.

This type of summary chart is typically 3 or 4 pages in length. The first column provides an abbreviated summary of the test findings. Compared with the full test report, this information is not as detailed but provides the gist of the test results. The second column provides information about how this child is likely to present in the classroom. It may include strengths as well as challenges that a teacher who is not familiar with the student might expect to see. The third column provides suggestions for educational interventions based on the evaluation findings. Typically, teachers (and parents as well) find this summary chart more relevant to their needs. It is also useful in situations in which a child has multiple teachers and the evaluator or parent would like each teacher to have a snapshot of the child's profile, needs, and intervention recommendations. This type of summary chart is not created *instead* of a traditional psychoeducational evaluation report. Rather, it is typically created *in addition to* the traditional report and is written specifically for teachers.

CHAPTER 8

How can parents get the most from the feedback meeting?

The feedback meeting with the evaluator and parents should be a time for discussing the test findings in a meaningful and understandable way. The goal is to educate parents, to relate the parents' initial concerns to the evaluation findings, and to make recommendations for teaching strategies, school placement and other interventions. If parents have established a good rapport with the evaluator, hopefully they are comfortable enough to share any worries they might have, any concerns that they did not share during the intake, and any questions that they have about recommendations. If next steps involve calling for an IEP meeting, parents may want to request that the evaluator accompany them to communicate the test findings to the school team and speak with other clinicians or teachers who are working with the child. However, the hope is that the feedback meeting contributes to helping the parents become knowledgeable about the test findings and making them feel more empowered to advocate for their child.

What contributes to a good feedback meeting?

- The initial diagnostic questions have been answered.

- Parents feel that they have a good understanding of the test findings and have the opportunity to have their questions answered.

- Parents feel they understand the implications of the testing for helping their child and have a good sense for next steps.

- If appropriate, the student also has a greater understanding of their strengths and challenges and has a sense for recommended strategies that will support learning.

Parents may find that the evaluation results are consistent with what they have observed with their child. However, the results should bring more clarity to the nature of the child's strengths and areas of difficulty as well as what interventions and supports would be helpful. For other parents, the findings may not be what they expected and they may need some time to absorb new and unexpected diagnoses and findings. The feedback meeting should be a time to go beyond diagnostic labels and discuss what these diagnoses mean in terms of intervention and supports that may be helpful. It is important to schedule enough time for the feedback meeting so parents do not feel rushed. Typically, a lot of information is presented, which takes some time to process fully. Parents should be provided with the opportunity to return or call with questions.

Parents may also need to know the limitations of testing. The evaluation is a measure of a child's functioning at one point in time. In that sense, it may not fully capture everything about how the child functions or learns. Results from younger children are not as stable as those from older students. Besides test scores, it is important to consider a child's strengths, how the child functions in school and in the community and what resources are available to support the child's development.

In addition, development and progress depend on many factors, and progress over time is not always predictable. Academic and social growth depend on the child receiving the right intervention, the appropriate intensity of intervention and the child's response to the intervention. Progress with children with complex needs may also depend on the ability to address a range of needs both at school and outside of school.

Should children receive feedback about their evaluation findings?

Providing feedback to students makes good sense, depending on the child's age and on parental preference. Many parents and many evaluators may feel that knowing IQ scores and other specific numbers is not beneficial to the student. However, there is always a way of providing feedback about strengths, challenges, and strategies to support learning in a manner that is age appropriate and helpful to the student. If this more general feedback to the student is felt to be appropriate, it may make sense to do a thorough feedback with all the scores and numbers with parents and then provide a different kind of feedback to the student.

How can parents use test findings to be considered for an IEP or a 504 plan in public school?

For some students who are in a public school setting, the report from the psychoeducational evaluation may be used as part of the consideration for special education services or accommodations. Sometimes, children will be evaluated at school by a school psychologist, special educator, or specialists such as a speech therapist or occupational therapist. However, parents are always entitled to pursue a private evaluation and the special education law requires that the public school team considers results from a private evaluation in planning for a child's needs. Parents can request an IEP (Individualized Educational Program) meeting, and if they have obtained a private evaluation, they should provide the report to the school in anticipation of this meeting. An IEP is typically authorized if a student meets certain criteria that qualify them for special education services.

The process of IEP consideration requires the student to meet certain criteria. In the school setting, there is usually first a review of how the student is doing in the regular classroom without specialized intervention. If the student is unable to make good academic progress with regular instruction, additional support is sometimes offered informally. However, if a student continues to struggle, the test findings are useful in determining the nature of the child's difficulty.

Children can qualify for special education services based on the nature of their primary disability. Obtaining an IEP requires that the child has a disability *and* that disability significantly impacts academic progress. The school will hold a team meeting with various educators, specialists, administrators, and parents. Parents are part of this decision-making team. If the team determines that the child has a disability that requires special education intervention, they will start by establishing a code to characterize the child's primary disability. There are thirteen possible codes which include the following:

- Specific Learning Disability
- Autism Spectrum Disorder
- Emotional Disability
- Speech or Language Impairment
- Visual Impairment
- Deafness
- Hearing Impairment
- Deaf-Blind
- Orthopedic Impairment
- Intellectual Disability
- Traumatic Brain Injury
- Multiple Disability
- Other Health Impairment.

Once the code has been determined, the child's current levels of functioning in academic skills, in social/behavioral functioning, and in cognitive skills related to learning are established. This information can be derived from the psychoeducational evaluation or from school-based assessments. Following this determination, goals are established in each area of need. Short- and long-term goals are developed, and these goals direct the intervention that will take place. Supplemental aids and services (classroom accommodations, instructional modifications, social/behavioral supports) are specified, and then the team determines what level of intervention will be provided. The IEP document includes the number of hours per week of special education services that will be provided either inside the regular classroom or outside of general education. It will also specify who the service providers will be. These providers can include learning specialists, reading specialists, speech and language therapists, occupational therapists, or other specialists. The IEP team is also mandated to consider the least restrictive environment (LRE) in which the child can learn. The special education law (IDEA) mandates that to the maximum extent possible, children should be educated within the mainstream classroom with non-disabled peers. Only after it has been determined that the least restrictive environment is not appropriate for meeting the child's needs can other special settings be discussed. Therefore, for many students, special education services will be provided in the mainstream classroom or with pull-out services from the regular classroom for specific intervention.

For some students who have a disability that does not require special education services, a 504 plan is sometimes developed. A 504 plan is different from an IEP in that the services are not provided by a special educator. Instead, it authorizes accommodations that are provided by the classroom teacher. It is often provided for students who need accommodations for ADHD, for anxiety or other emotional issues or for health issues.

Once the IEP or the 504 plan has been developed, the next step is to make sure that the intervention plan is implemented in a way that is beneficial to the student. The goals and methods identified in the IEP or 504 plan provide a guide and criteria against which parents and school personnel can monitor progress. For this reason, it is important that the child's needs are carefully addressed in the IEP or 504 plan. Typically, an IEP or 504 plan is set up to span a calendar year, but parents can call for a review meeting at any time they feel the need or if they have concerns about their child's progress.

Would a private school option be better?

At times, parents may want to consider private school options for meeting their child's learning needs. For some children, a mainstream private school with a smaller student-to-teacher ratio may be sufficient to address some needs that their child may have for more individualized attention. For other students, parents may want the expertise of a very specialized school for children with learning challenges. Exploring the specialized techniques and educational interventions that these schools offer may be attractive to parents seeking specific types of supports for their child. Often the intensity of intervention services in a specialized private school is greater than what is provided in public school. Sometimes, the whole structure of the instruction has a different focus which parents may feel would benefit their child. For example, a school for students with language-based learning disabilities may provide an environment with an emphasis on visual supports or hands-on learning that may benefit students with certain learning profiles. A school that has an emphasis on social skill development may provide a social skills curriculum that is integrated throughout the school day.

As parents consider the option for private school placement, the results from the psychoeducational evaluation are often very beneficial to use when evaluating how that setting could address the identified needs. These specialized private schools often require parents to provide diagnostic testing to see if their setting is an appropriate match and as a way to inform educational planning. Often, with the diagnostic information in hand, parents and admissions staff can better evaluate whether the school is a good fit. Private school options are more costly, but many also have financial aid available for families who may need it. Some students can also be funded by the public school system if they are not able to address the student's IEP needs.

CHAPTER 9

How can parents best advocate for their child's needs after the evaluation?

Building your advocacy skills

Becoming your child's advocate is a process that grows with experience. Parents who are just beginning with their child's first formal evaluation are at the beginning stages of becoming an advocate. Yet even at this point, you are the expert in your child's development. You know the history. You know your child's strengths and challenges. You have a sense of your child's developmental trajectory over time. The evaluator may have certain expertise that you need and may be knowledgeable about diagnostics, about child development and about the educational process, but ultimately you want to work together as a team.

As your child's advocate, you will have the opportunity to contribute to and learn from the evaluation process. The evaluator will hopefully educate you so that you can advocate for your child. Initially you are providing developmental information to the evaluator, and the evaluator, in turn, is providing certain diagnostic information to you. You may need to understand more about tests and what they measure, how to interpret the testing that has taken place, and how to use the information to help meet your child's needs. The better this information is explained and the better the discussion at the feedback meeting, the better you will ultimately be in understanding your child and discussing their needs with others. An evaluation with good parent feedback should leave parents feeling more knowledgeable about their child and more able to advocate for them.

What are some options if you feel the need for an outside advocate?

In many cases, after the feedback meeting, parents will feel confident that they understand their child's needs and can advocate for their child at a school meeting. However, at times, parents may feel the need for additional support when meeting with their child's school team to develop intervention planning or to find a new school placement for their child. There are generally three levels of support that parents may want to consider: having the evaluator accompany them to the IEP meeting, hiring an educational advocate or hiring a special education attorney.

Involving the evaluator in the IEP meeting

Parents may prefer to have the evaluator present at the IEP meeting to interpret the evaluation to the school-based team members and to advocate for the child's needs based on the evaluation recommendations. Parents may also feel more comfortable with the evaluator sitting with them at this meeting. The psychologist who did the evaluation is uniquely qualified to interpret the results to the rest of the team.

Using an educational advocate

An educational advocate typically has expertise in special education law and education. As a result, the advocate can be useful during the IEP process by helping parents understand the law and by ensuring that the process of consideration for an IEP and the IEP itself is developed appropriately. The IEP planning process can be intimidating to parents, and they are

63

sometimes surprised when they arrive at the meeting to see a long conference table with eight or more professionals, including educators, a school psychologist, administrators, and other specialists. Parents may feel overwhelmed by educational and legal jargon. They may be uncomfortable fielding questions and comments from the rest of the team or unable to answer technical questions about a private psychoeducational evaluation. Educational advocates can accompany parents to the IEP or 504 meeting and can support parents by helping to interpret the test report to the rest of the team and by making sure that the process is fair and that the child's needs are adequately addressed by the IEP document.

Hiring a special education attorney

A special education attorney is a resource that parents may want to consider, particularly if there has been some contentiousness or disagreement about how to address their child's needs, about a decision to deny an IEP or about how the child's needs have been addressed after the IEP has been developed. There are times when a public school setting is not able to meet the child's needs as defined in an IEP. The special education law provides for the option to consider private placements if the public school cannot meet the child's needs. At times, a special education attorney can help parents document when a school has not met its obligation or has not met a child's needs. It is not always necessary to hire an attorney to make this case, but at times, parents may feel the need to hire an attorney if they feel they are not able to negotiate their concerns with the school themselves. Parents may also choose to consult with an attorney before an IEP meeting for guidance, without having them attend the meeting.

Typically, parents grow in their ability to advocate for their child with more experience meeting with school personnel, more familiarity with testing and more appreciation for what does and does not work for their child. If you are just starting the process, know that as with all other new learning, you start as a novice and become an expert over time.

CHAPTER 10

Frequently asked questions (FAQs)

If my child takes medication for ADHD, should
it be taken during the evaluation?

Typically, the answer to this question is yes. If a child with ADHD is already using medication, then the goal of the evaluation is to assess how the child learns given the medication that is currently being used. The child's attention issues may not be entirely controlled by medication, and the child may continue to exhibit some attention or executive function skill weaknesses that impact academic achievement. It is important to adjust medication to cover the time when the testing will occur. If the child is tested on different days at different times of day, the parent should be sure that medication is used in a similar manner on each day of testing. Testing some days on medication and some days without is likely to produce confusing test findings. It is helpful to discuss the use of medication for ADHD during the evaluation with the psychologist.

I hear the term *executive function skills*. What
does that mean and how is it evaluated?

There have been many attempts to define executive function skills and there is no agreed upon definition of this term. McCloskey, Perkins and Van Divner (2009), define it as "a set of multiple cognitive abilities that direct a child's ability to engage in purposeful, organized, strategic, self-regulated, goal-directed, processing of perceptions, emotions, thoughts and actions" (p. 15). Drs. Gioia, Isquith, Guy and Kenworthy (2000) have identified 8 executive function skills, which are measured in the BRIEF2, which is the questionnaire they have developed to assess these skills. They include inhibition (the ability to stop one's behavior at the appropriate time), shift (the ability to move flexibly from one situation to another and to think flexibly), self-monitoring (the ability to be aware of one's own behavior and how it impacts others). emotional control (the ability to regulate emotional responses), initiation (the ability to begin a task and to generate ideas, responses or problem solving strategies independently), working memory (the ability to hold information in mind and to maintain focus in order to complete a task), planning/organization (the ability to plan out and carry out task demands), and organization of materials (the ability to keep track of one's things). Executive function skills are measured indirectly by having parents, teachers or students complete questionnaires that measure these functions. Clinicians also evaluate executive function skills by direct observation of these skills during the testing process. In addition, there are some formal measures of executive function skills on tests such as the NEPSY II and the D-KEFS. There is no formal DSM-V diagnosis of executive function skill weakness, although clinicians often speak to it in their evaluation findings and see it as related to ADHD.

How is a psychoeducational evaluation different from a neuropsychological evaluation?

This is a frequently asked question that is often confusing to parents. In the past (and sometimes currently) neuropsychological evaluations were felt to be broader in scope than psychoeducational evaluations. However, this is not necessarily true. A neuropsychologist may focus more often on cognitive processing and executive function skills such as memory, attention, organization, and the ability to regulate behavior, and sometimes focus less on education and academic assessment. However, many psychologists who conduct comprehensive psychoeducational evaluations use many of these same measures and may also have a greater emphasis on in-depth educational assessments. So, the answer is that there is a great deal of overlap depending on the evaluator. A neuropsychological evaluation is likely to be more appropriate if there are concerns after a potential brain injury. A neuropsychological evaluation is also more likely to interpret findings in terms of brain function. However, those clinicians doing comprehensive psychoeducational evaluations frequently make these connections as well. A more important question when seeking out either a neuropsychological evaluation or a psychoeducational evaluation is how in-depth the assessment will be and what aspects of the assessment will be included.

My child recently had an evaluation that I did not think was valid. Can I redo the evaluation with a new evaluator?

It is customary not to repeat many tests within a certain period of time. The reason for this is to prevent the child from having a practice effect - that is, remembering and having practice with the test items. This practice effect undermines the validity of the test. Typically, IQ measures are not repeated within the year. However, if there was a reason that the test was felt to be invalid, perhaps because the child was sick or behaviorally unwilling to engage with the examiner, there may be a need to get more valid measures of ability or achievement. Thankfully, achievement tests often come in different parallel forms, which allows the examiner to give a different form of the test. For IQ tests, this is not the case. However, it is possible to give a different IQ test that has not been previously used.

Can the evaluation measure my child's progress over time?

Evaluations measure the child's abilities and skills at one point in time, characterizing their scores relative to peers in different areas of cognitive processing and achievement. Retesting the child after a specific time period can provide a better sense for progress over time. If a child earns a standard score on an achievement test of 90 at the initial testing, that score indicates that the child is at the 25th percentile relative to peers in that skill at that point in time. A year later, the normative group of peers has made a year's progress. If the child earns a score of 90 on the same test after a year, that indicates that the child has made a year's progress as has the peer group. As a result, the child has made a year's progress but has earned the same score. If the child's score at the second testing is 100 (50th percentile), that indicates that the child has made more than a year's progress and this is an indicator that the child is making up the delay observed at the initial testing. If a child's score drops a year later, it indicates that their rate of progress is slower than their peers and indicates that they are now weaker relative to peers than previously. It is this initial testing and the follow up testing that provide a measure of whether a student's delays continue or resolve over time. At times, grade-level scores can be a more useful metric and can demonstrate that at point A the student was functioning at the second grade level in reading, and at point B the student is now functioning at the fourth grade level. Understanding progress over time can be important in evaluating whether planned interventions have been effective.

Will my child's test results be different after starting ADHD medication?

The answer is sometimes yes. The testing process often involves challenging the child with items that become increasingly difficult. Children who don't have the patience or focus to take apart more difficult problems or to stay with a difficult problem long enough to solve it may tend to quickly give up or to guess impulsively rather than working out a problem systematically. As a result, they may earn lower scores. Once attention is better controlled, there are often improvements in scores to the degree that focus is the reason for the lower score. Using ADHD medication over a period of time may also result in improved test scores because the student has been better able to take in academic instruction in the classroom and master learning strategies that also result in better test scores. It may make sense to retest a child the following year after using medication for a while to see if their performance improves.

If an academic weakness is identified, how do I know if this is something that my child will struggle with for many years or if it will resolve over time?

This question is hard to answer, particularly for younger children who are having their initial evaluation. There are elementary school students who have a slow start to reading in kindergarten, but then by second grade seem to take off with reading and remain at grade level. Other students who are identified with a reading delay in first grade will continue to show delays relative to peers when tested in third or fifth grade. The way to begin to answer this question is to test early and then retest after a year or two. Children whose standard scores improve from one testing to the next demonstrate that they are closing the gap they initially had relative to peers. In the meantime, it is best to provide the most appropriate intervention and to then assess how the child has responded to that intervention.

My child has scored lower on IQ tests with each additional administration. Why would this be?

Children who exhibit developmental delays are sometimes gaining cognitive abilities or academic skills at a slower rate than their peers. Since IQ scores are based on comparing a child with same-age peers, this slower growth rate over time will result in lower and lower scores. However, these standard scores do not reflect progress, which may be significant. To get a better idea of progress, it may be more important to quantify grade-level progress from year to year. For example, a student may be functioning at the second grade level in reading initially and after a year be functioning at the fourth grade level. Although this may be lower than the child's grade-level norms, it does represent significant progress and may be indicative that intervention strategies are working well.

My child's writing skills in high school are weak. However, when she was tested with the Woodcock Johnson IV, measures of written expression, she scored in the Average range. Why would this be?

This is a good example of the need to look at whether tests that appear to be measuring writing are specific enough to address a particular area of concern. The Woodcock Johnson IV Writing Sample subtest requires students to respond to specific sentence-writing prompts, which are scored based on the ideas expressed in these sentences. There are no demands for open-ended writing, such as writing an essay, and responses are not scored for writing mechanics such as spelling, punctuation, capitalization, or handwriting. It may be that the student is able to do these very structured, brief, sentence-writing tasks but cannot generate ideas independently for an essay or organize an essay. The student may also demonstrate weaknesses in spelling, handwriting, punctuation, and capitalization. If these factors are not measured by the writing test given, there is missing diagnostic information that can only be answered by choosing a writing test that taps these areas of weakness.

How do I prioritize all the intervention strategies suggested for my child?

Many excellent evaluations provide numerous suggestions for intervention and support. When developing school-based interventions, parents typically want the school to implement as many suggestions as possible with appropriate intensity.

There may also be many suggestions made about interventions and supports parents can provide outside of school. In this area, families must make decisions about creating a schedule for their child that is not too intense on the one hand and yet will help their child grow. For children who are quite tired and spent after a day at school, having outside-of-school therapy appointments three to four times a week may be too much. This really depends on their age, maturity and how they manage all these interventions. If the intensity of interventions seems too high, prioritizing the activities may be essential. Parents may want to consider whether some interventions should be prioritized because they are not provided in school. Parents may also feel that at a certain point in time, the priority should be on developing reading or writing skills because these are felt to be most important to student's current school progress. Some parents choose to do intensive summer programs at a time when there are no competing school demands. In addition, there may be financial or logistical considerations that may be important to take into consideration.

The test results indicate that my child has a learning disability, but the school says he is functioning within the Average range and does not want to provide supports. Can they deny services?

Schools sometimes use the Response to Intervention (RTI) model to determine which children should receive special education services or be provided with accommodations or supports in the classroom. RTI is a three-tier model that starts with Tier 1, which is high quality, evidence-based regular classroom instruction. If students are struggling academically at this level, they are provided with Tier 2 interventions which are more intensive and provided in small groups. If students continue to struggle at this level, Tier 3 provides individualized intervention, which may include referral for an IEP. However, at any point in the RTI process, IDEA allows parents to request a formal evaluation to determine eligibility for special education. If the child is earning passing grades, this is sometimes used by the schools as a reason not to provide special services. However, students can earn good grades and yet show evidence of ADHD or a learning disability. The law requires schools to provide a free, appropriate education (FAPE) to any child with a disability who needs special education even though the child has not failed or been retained in a course or grade and is advancing from grade to grade. The US Department of Education Office for Civil Rights addressed this in 2016 in a paper addressing eligibility of students with ADHD for a 504 plan and indicated "It is critical to reject the assumption that an individual who has performed well academically cannot be substantially limited in activities such as learning, reading, writing, thinking or speaking. The school districts should ask how difficult it is or how much time it takes for a student with ADHD in comparison to a student without ADHD to plan, begin, complete or turn in an essay, term paper, homework assignment or exam." That document also indicates that it is not appropriate to deny a disability because of mitigating factors in place such as the use of medication or behavioral interventions for ADHD. (Students with ADHD and Section 504: A Resource Guide, 2016).

FINAL THOUGHTS

A comprehensive psychoeducational evaluation, done well, can be very beneficial in understanding the nature of a learning difficulty, in helping the child's school better meet their needs, and in helping parents become better advocates for their child. This book provides an orientation to the psychoeducational evaluation process. Not all elements may need to be included in any specific evaluation. However, this book has been written to help parents know the range of options that are available and become more knowledgeable about the process. To the degree that parents understand what's involved, they can become more comfortable about beginning the process and can participate more fully as a team with the evaluator and their child's teacher in developing effective approaches for teaching and learning.

APPENDIX OF TESTS

The following list provides a sample of commonly used tests of cognitive abilities, academic skills, attention, and social/emotional factors, as well as commonly used questionnaire measures. This list is not meant to be exhaustive and does not capture the full range of tests that are available. However, the tests are listed to give parents an introduction to some of tests that may be suggested as part of their child's evaluation.

Tests of cognitive abilities

Bayley Scales of Infant and Toddler Development - Third Edition
What it is used for: To assess intellectual, motor, language, adaptive behavior, and emotional development.
Age range: 1 month through 42 months

Comprehensive Test of Nonverbal Intelligence (CTONI) – Second Edition (CTONI-2)
What it is used for: To assess nonverbal intelligence without demands for language.
Age range: 6 years through 90 years

Detroit Tests of Learning Aptitude - Fifth Edition (DTLA-5)
What it is used for: To assess general intelligence and specific cognitive abilities.
Age range: 6 years through 17 years, 11 months

Differential Ability Scales - Second Edition (DAS-II)

What it is used for: To assess children's cognitive ability with minimal influence from culture. Assesses verbal, nonverbal, and spatial abilities.

Age range: 2 years, 6 months through 17 years, 11 months

Kaufman Assessment Battery for Children - Second Edition (KABC-II)

What it is used for: To assess intellectual functioning.

Age range: 3 years through 18 years

Leiter International Performance Scale - Third Edition (Leiter-3)

What it is used for: Provides a nonverbal measure of assessing intelligence for use with those who are cognitively delayed, non-English speaking, hearing impaired, speech impaired, or on the autism spectrum. Directions are modeled.

Age range: 3 years through 75 years

NEPSY - Second Edition (NEPSY-II)

What it is used for: To measure cognitive abilities related to learning including language skills, attention/executive-function skills, sensorimotor skills, visual-spatial skills, memory and learning skills, visual spatial skills and social perception.

Age range: 3 years through 16 years

Scholastic Aptitude Test for Adults (SATA)

What it is used for: To measure cognitive abilities in the areas of verbal and nonverbal abilities, quantitative reasoning, vocabulary, as well as academic achievement in reading, math, and writing under timed conditions.

Age range: 16 years to 70 years

Stanford-Binet Intelligence Scales - Fifth Edition (SB5)
What it is used for: To assess intellectual functioning.
Age range: 2 years to 85 years

Test of Nonverbal Intelligence - Fourth Edition (TONI-4)
What it is used for: To assess intellectual functioning without demands for language.
Age range: 6 years through 89 years

Wechsler Abbreviated Scale of Intelligence - Second Edition (WASI-II)
What it is used for: To create a brief measure of intellectual functioning.
Age range: 6 years through 85 years

Wechsler Adult Intelligence Scale - Fourth Edition (WAIS-IV)
What it is used for: To assess cognitive abilities in areas related to language, visual-spatial skills, fluid reasoning, working memory, and processing speed.
Age range: 16 years through 90 years

Wechsler Intelligence Scale for Children - Fifth Edition (WISC-V)
What it is used for: To assess cognitive abilities in areas related to language, visual-spatial skills, fluid reasoning, working memory, and processing speed.
Age range: 6 years to 15 years, 11 months

Wechsler Intelligence Scale for Children - Fifth Edition – Integrated (WISC-V, Integrated)
What it is used for: To provide deeper understanding of cognitive processes impacting a child's WISC-V performance.
Age range: 6 years, 0 months to 16 years, 11 months

Wechsler Preschool and Primary Scale of Intelligence - Fourth Edition (WPPSI-IV)

What it is used for: To assess cognitive abilities in areas related to language, visual-spatial skills, fluid reasoning, working memory, and processing speed.

Age range: 2 years, 6 months to 7 years, 7 months

Wechsler Nonverbal Scale of Ability (WNV)

What it is used for: To assess intellectual functioning without demands for language.

Age range: 4 years through 21 years, 11 months

Woodcock Johnson IV Test of Cognitive Abilities

What it is used for: To measure a wide range of cognitive abilities.

Age range: 2 years to adult

Tests of specific cognitive abilities

Beery Test of Visual Motor Integration - Sixth Edition (Beery VMI)

What it is used for: To measure skills in visual-motor integration, visual perception, and fine-motor control

Age range: 2 years to adult

Children's Memory Scales (CMS)

What it is used for: To assess various aspects of memory in children.

Age range: 5 years to 16 years

Clinical Evaluation of Language Fundamentals - Fifth Edition (CELF-5)

What it is used for: To assess language skills in areas related to language comprehension, language formulation, pragmatics, vocabulary, and reading comprehension.

Age range: 5 years through 21 years

Clinical Evaluation of Language Fundamentals - Fifth Edition - Metalinguistics (CELF-5, Metalinguistics)

What it is used for: To evaluate higher-level language skills in the areas of language pragmatics and language semantics.

Age range: 9 to 21 years, 11 months

Comprehensive Test of Phonological Processing - Second Edition (CTOPP2)

What it is used for: To assess underlying cognitive abilities related to reading, including phonological awareness, phonological memory, and rapid-naming skills.

Age range: 4 years through 24 years

OWLS-II Tests of Listening Comprehension and Oral Expression

What it is used for: To evaluate skills in processing language and in language formulation.

Age range: 5 year to 21 years

Peabody Picture Vocabulary Test - Fourth Edition (PPVT-4)

What it is used for: To assess one word receptive and expressive vocabulary knowledge.

Age range: 2 years, 6 months through 90+

Rey Complex Figure Test (RCFT)

What it is used for: To measure the child's visual-motor constructional ability and visual-spatial organizational skills. Recall and recognition can also be measured.

Age range: 6 years through 89 years

Wechsler Memory Scale - Fourth Edition (WMS-IV)

What it is used for: To assess aspects of verbal, visual, and working memory.

Age range: 16 years to 90 years

Wide Range Assessment of Memory and Learning - Second Edition (WRAML2)

What it is used for: To measure verbal and visual memory skills as well as working memory skills.

Age range: 5 years through to 90 years

Woodcock Johnson IV Test of Oral Language

What it is used for: To measure skills in oral expression, listening comprehension, phonetic coding, vocabulary, and speed of lexical access.

Age range: 2 years to 90 years

General tests of academic achievement

Kaufman Test of Educational Achievement - Third Edition (K-TEA-3)

What it is used for: To measure achievement in reading, writing, and math.

Age range: 4 years to 25 years, 11 months

Wechsler Individual Achievement Test – Fourth Edition (WIAT-IV)

What it is used for: To measure reading, writing, and math skills, as well as some skills in listening comprehension and oral expression.

Age range: Preschool through age 50

Woodcock Johnson IV Test of Achievement (WJ IV Achievement)

What it is used for: Tests general achievement in reading, writing, and math.

Age range: Preschool through college

Single-subject tests of achievement

Feifer Assessment of Math (FAM)

What it is used for: To diagnose and assess possible math learning disability in areas related to procedural weaknesses, verbal weaknesses, or semantic weaknesses.

Age range: Preschool through college

Feifer Assessment of Reading (FAR)

What it is used for: To diagnose and assess possible reading disability in areas related to phonological awareness, fluency, and comprehension.

Age range: Preschool through college

Feifer Assessment of Writing (FAW)

What it is used for: To diagnose and assess possible learning disability in written expression or dysgraphia.

Age range: Preschool through college

Gray Oral Reading Test - Fifth Edition (GORT5)

What it is used for: To measure oral reading accuracy, fluency and reading comprehension.

Age range: 6 years through 23 years, 11 months

Gray Silent Reading Test (GSRT),

What it is used for: To measure silent reading comprehension ability.

Age range: 7 years to 25 years

Key Math Diagnostic Assessment - Third Edition (KeyMath3)

What it is used for: To comprehensively assess math skills.

Age range: 4 years, 5 months through 23 years

Nelson-Denny Reading Test, Forms I and J (NDRT)

What it is used for: To measure reading comprehension and vocabulary knowledge under timed conditions.

Age range: 16 years to college

Oral and Written Language Scales - Second Edition (OWLS-II) Tests of Reading Comprehension and Written Expression

What it is used for: To measure reading comprehension and written expression.

Age range: 5 years to 21 years

Process Assessment of the Learner - Second Edition (PAL-II)

What it is used for: To assess cognitive processes involved in academic skills related to reading, writing and math.

Age range: kindergarten through sixth grade

Scholastic Aptitude Test for Adults (SATA)

What it is used for: To measure reading comprehension, written expression, math calculation, math application skills under timed conditions.

Age range: 16 years through adult

Test of Early Mathematics Ability - Third Edition (TEMA-3)

What it is used for: To assess math performance in young children.

Age range: 3 years to 8 years, 11 months

Test of Word Reading Efficiency - Second Edition (TOWRE-2)
What it is used for: To measure sight word reading fluency.
Age range: 6 years to 24 years, 11 months

Test of Written Language - Fourth Edition (TOWL-4)
What it is used for: To evaluate written language skills in areas of vocabulary, spelling, punctuation, sentence-combining skills, and editing skills.
Age range: 9 years through 17 years, 11 months

Woodcock Reading Mastery Tests - Third Edition (WRMT-III)
What it is used for: To assess reading readiness, basic reading skills, and word/passage comprehension.
Age range: 5 years through 75 years

Computer-based tests of attention

Conners Continuous Performance Test - Second Edition (CPT-2)
What it is used for: to measure attention and inhibitory control.
Age range: 6 years and up

Connors Kiddie Continuous Performance Test - Second Edition (K-CPT2)
What it is used for: To measure attention, impulsivity, sustained attention, and vigilance.
Age: 4 years to 7 years

Integrated Visual and Auditory Continuous Performance Test - Second Edition (IVA-2 CPT)
What it is used for: To assess variables related to attention and response-control functioning.
Age range: 6 years to 96 years

Test of Variables of Attention (T.O.V.A.)

What it is used for: To measure variables related to attention.

Age range: 4 years to 80+ years

Tests of social/emotional factors

Autism Diagnostic Observation Schedule - Second Edition (ADOS-2)

What it is used for: Provides a semi-structured, standardized assessment of communication, social interaction, play, and restricted and repetitive behaviors.

Age range: 12 months to adulthood

House/Tree/Person

What it is used for: A projective drawing task to assess emotional factors.

Age range: 3 years and up

Robert's Apperception Test for Children – 2 (Roberts-2)

What it is used for: To assess social perceptions of children.

Age range: 6 years to 18 years

Rorschach Inkblot Test

What it is used for: To evaluate personality characteristics and emotional functioning.

Age range: 5 years to adult

Test of Problem Solving - Second Edition – Adolescent (TOPS -2)

What it is used for: To assess critical thinking ability and social problem-solving.

Age range: 12 years to 17 years, 11 months

Test of Problem Solving - Second Edition – Elementary (TOPS – 3: E)

What it is used for: To assess critical thinking ability and social problem-solving.

Age range: 6 years to 12 years

Questionnaire measures

Adaptive Behavior Assessment System - Third Edition (ABAS-3)

What it is used for: To assess skills in the areas of communication, community use, health and safety and self-direction.

Age range: birth through 89 years

Behavior Assessment System for Children -Third Edition (BASC3)

What it is used for: To assess social skills and behavior in areas related to externalizing problems, internalizing problems, positive social skills, and attention.

Age range: 2 years to 21 years, 11 months

Behavior Rating Inventory of Executive Functions - Second Edition (BRIEF2)

What it is used for: To measure executive function skills in areas related to behavioral regulation, emotional regulation, and cognitive regulation.

Age range: Preschool through college and adult

Brown Attention - Deficit Disorder Scales

What it is used for: To screen for Inattentive type and Hyperactive/Impulsive type ADHD.

Age range: 3 years through adult

Children's Depression Inventory (CDI)

What it is used for: To assess symptoms of depression in children and adults.

Age range: 7 years to 17 years

Conners 3 Early Childhood (Conners EC)

What it is used for: To measure factors related to attention, behavior, and development.

Age range: 2 years to 6 years

Conners 3 Parent and Teacher Rating Scales

What it is used for: To measure factors related to Inattentive type ADHD, Hyperactive/Impulsive type ADHD, learning problems, and behavioral problems.

Age range: 6 years to 18 years

Gilliam Autism Rating Scale - Second Edition (GARS-2)

What it is used for: To screen for symptoms related to autism.

Age range: 3 years to 22 years

Revised Childhood Manifest Anxiety Scale - Second Edition (RCMAS-2)

What it is used for: A self-report assessment to measure the level and nature of anxiety.

Age range: 6 years to 19 years

Social Responsiveness Scale - Second Edition (SRS-II)

What it is used for: To identify the presence and severity of social impairment. Measures five factors along a continuum from typical behavior to autism. Factors measured include social awareness, social cognition, social communication, social motivation, and autistic behaviors.

Age range: 2 years, 5 months to adulthood

Vineland Adaptive Behavior Scales -Third Edition (Vineland-3)

What it is used for: To assess skills in the areas of communication, daily-living skills, and socialization.

Age range: birth through 90 years

REFERENCES

Bray, B. and McClaskey, K. (2017). *How to Personalize Learning: A Practical Guide for Getting Started and Going Deeper,* Thousand Oaks, CA: Corwin.

Feifer, S. (2013). *The Neuropsychology of Written Language Disorders: A Framework for Effective Interventions,* Middletown, MD: School Neuropsych Press.

Feifer, S. (2017). *The Neuropsychology of Mathematics: An Introduction to the FAM,* Middleton, MD: School Neuropsych Press.

Feifer, S. and De Fina, P. (2000). *The Neuropsychology of Reading Disorders: Diagnosis and Intervention Workbook,* Middletown, MD: School Neuropsych Press.

Gioia, G. A., Isquith, P. K., Guy, S. C., and Kenworthy, L. (2000). *Behavior rating inventory of executive function: Professional manual.* Lutz, FL: Psychological Assessment Resources.

Goldberg, E. (2001). *The Executive Brain: Frontal Lobes and the Civilized Mind,* New York: Oxford University Press.

Hale, J. and Fiorello, C. (2004) *School Neuropsychology: A Practitioner's Handbook,* New York: Guilford Press.

McCloskey, G., Perkins, L., and Van Divner, B. (2009). *Assessment and Intervention for Executive Function Difficulties*, New York: Taylor and Francis Group.

Standard Scores. Retrieved from: https://www.assessingpsych.wordpress.com/psychometrics/page/2/.

US Department of Education, Office of Civil Rights, *Students with ADHD, and Section 504: A Resource Guide*, (July, 2016).